PICKING APPLES

by Finley Fraser

Consultant: Beth Gambro
Reading Specialist, Yorkville, Illinois

BEARPORT
PUBLISHING

Minneapolis, Minnesota

Teaching Tips

Before Reading

- Discuss the different seasons. What happens in fall?

- Look through the glossary together. Read and discuss the words.

- Go on a picture walk, looking through the pictures to discuss vocabulary and make predictions about the text.

During Reading

- Encourage readers to point to each word as it is read. Stop occasionally to ask readers to point to a specific word in the text.

- If a reader encounters an unknown word, ask them to look at the rest of the page. Are there any clues to help them understand?

After Reading

- Check for understanding.

  ▸ What kind of trees grow apples?

  ▸ What treats can you make with apples? What kinds of apples might you use for each treat?

- Ask the readers to think deeper.

  ▸ Look at page 22. Do you think you could grow an apple tree at your home? Why or why not?

Credits:
Cover © JP Chretien/Shutterstock; 3, © Valery121283/Shutterstock; 5, © ericmichaud/iStock; 6, © Zheltyshev/Shutterstock; 7, © Lya_Cattel/iStock; 8, © xpixel/Shutterstock; 9, © filmfoto/iStock; 10, © Slatan/Shutterstock; 12, © PicturePartners/iStock; 14, © PumpizoldA/iStock; 15, © SDI Productions/iStock; 17, © pilipphoto/Shutterstock; 18, © Mshev/Shutterstock; 19, © FamStudio/Shutterstock; 20, © phototropic/iStock; 21, © Tetra Images - Pauline St.Denis/Getty Images; 22, © pixelnest/Shutterstock; 22, © Fahkamram/Shutterstock; 22, © Petr Levicek/Shutterstock; 22, © Masterovoy/Shutterstock; 23, © leopictures/Shutterstock; 23, © catalina.m/Shutterstock; 23, © bhofack2/iStock; 23, © Elena Veselova/Shutterstock; 24, © Iurii Kachkovskyi/Shutterstock.

Library of Congress Cataloging-in-Publication Data

Names: Fraser, Finley, 1972- author.
Title: Picking apples / by Finley Fraser.
Description: Bearcub books. | Minneapolis, Minnesota : Bearport Publishing Company, 2020. | Series: Seasons of fun: fall | Includes bibliographical references and index.
Identifiers: LCCN 2020014855 (print) | LCCN 2020014856 (ebook) | ISBN 9781642809350 (library binding) | ISBN 9781642809428 (paperback) | ISBN 9781642809497 (ebook)
Subjects: LCSH: Apples—Juvenile literature. | Orchards-Juvenile literature. | Autumn—Juvenile literature.
Classification: LCC SB363 .F76 2020 (print) | LCC SB363 (ebook) | DDC 634/.11—dc23
LC record available at https://lccn.loc.gov/2020014855
LC ebook record available at https://lccn.loc.gov/2020014856

For more information, write to Bearport Publishing, 5357 Penn Avenue South, Minneapolis, MN 55419.

Printed in the United States of America.

Contents

Picking Apples

It is time for fall fun!

Today, we are going apple picking.

I am going to pick lots of apples!

We go to a big farm.

It has lots of
apple trees.

The trees are planted
in long rows.

I see so many apples on the trees!

How did they get there?

In spring, the trees were full of pretty flowers.

Then, tiny apples started to grow.

The trees needed lots of sun for the apples to grow big.

The apples are ready now that it is fall.

There are many kinds of apples.

Some apples are red.

Some are green.

Some are even yellow!

We fill a **basket** with apples.

We pick different kinds.

I like the green apples best.

Yum!

At home, we make lots of apple **treats**.

We make apple pie from green apples.

It is my favorite!

Apple cake

We use red and green apples to make apple cake, too.

Then, we make **applesauce**.

This time, we use yellow apples.

Applesauce

Picking apples is fun.

It's one of the best things to do in fall!

How Apples Grow

Apple trees grow flowers in the spring.

The flowers have **pollen**. Bees spread pollen from flower to flower as they eat.

Then, the flowers fall off the trees and tiny apples start to grow. The apples grow for months. They are ready in the fall.

Glossary

applesauce a sweet sauce made by cooking apples until they are soft

basket something used for carrying things

pollen the yellow powder in flowers that plants use to make new plants

treats foods that are tasty to eat

Index

Read More

Brannon, Cecelia H. *Apples (All About Food Crops).* New York: Enslow Publishing (2018).

Merrick, Gabriel. *We Pick Apples (I Live on a Farm).* New York: PowerKids Press (2018).

Learn More Online

1. Go to **www.factsurfer.com**
2. Enter "**Picking Apples**" into the search box.
3. Click on the cover of this book to see a list of websites.

About the Author

Finley Fraser loves picking apples in the fall. Apple pie is his favorite food!